WHO OPENS

WHO OPENS

Jesse Seldess

Kenning Editions, 2006

for Gail, Mark, and Zachary Seldess

Everything is foreseen, yet freedom of choice is granted.

The Talmud

Hum With

Who you have continually overheard
Had your body
Been chorus overheard
Had your
To strength in security hands
Had your permission
Been harmonized appeal
To your look through hearing
Had been
Without end acted on
Internally to you

Hum With

Without end acted on

Had skin
Been eternally to you

Had been
Without end acted on
Internally to you

Internalized to you

Through your look to hearing
Had been
Without end acted on
Mentalized to you

Motorized to you

Vocalized to you

Through your look to hearing
Had been
Without end acted on
Inverted to you

Had skin
Without end acted on
Been realized to you

cauterized to you

Without end acted on

Had skin
Been motorized to you
Without end acted on

Had skin
Been cauterized to you
Without end acted on

Had focus
Without end acted on
Been offset with color

Been made up with

Offset acted on

Been acted upon

Been

color

Had your body
Been chorus overheard
Had your

Had your permission
Been harmonized appeal

Without end acted on
Had focus
Been offset color

Been turnip covered

Through your look to hearing
Had focus
Been without end acted on

Had your body
Been chorus overheard

To look up
Through your look to hearing
Had focus
Been without end acted on

To look up

Rendering
Up

Register

But all acted on

Had focus
Been without end
But all acted on

overend
Describe acted on

Described without and
Acted on

Would circumscribe
Been end acted on

Been to circumscribe
Without end act on

Had focus
Been to circumscribe
Without end act on

Had focus
Been without
End acted on

Been circumscribed
Been described
End without

without grasping
To end acted on

grasp

grasping describe
Without end acted on

Had focus
Been circumscribed
Without end act on

Had focus
Been circumscribe
Without end act on
without
End to acted upon
Without end act upon

Been circumscribed without
End to acted upon
Without end act upon

To
rightened your
Been gasping without end

Had heightened
Been focus without end

Acted on

Without end acted on
Had your
Been without end
To acted upon

Had focus
Been without end

Droned

Droned focus
Had focus
Been without end

Been harmonized appeal
Inflected on
To your look through hearing
Had focus
Been without end

Remembered end
Had your permission

Been end acting

Remembered and acted on

Acting memory

Been without end
Acting in mind

To acting on flair

Had focus
Been without end
To acting on hook
acted on
To your mind

And urging

urge

acted on

Been acting on
Without end

To acting on

End acted on

Act on

body
End acted on

Been without your body
To end acted on

Had focus
Been without faculty
To end acted on

remembered end acted on

End acting on

To end acted on
Had your look through hearing

To look up end acted on

To look up
To end acted on

To look up
To please
End acted on

Bright remembered
End acted on

bright
Had your
ly met
your
End acted upon

To look up
To

Had your grasping permission
To look up
To harmonized appeal

Remembered end acted upon

Had your gasping harmonized
To appeal

Had your permission
Been harmonized
Looking up to appeal

Remembered end acted upon
Had your moving harmonized
Been permission to look up

For grasping open your
Your permission to look up

Had your moving

Been appealing to look up
urge

Appealing to look up to

Urging

Been urging appeal

Appeal

Harmonized

Appealing

Had your moving omission

Had your moving harmonized
Been appealing

Had your moving omission
Been harmonized

Had your moving appeal
Harmonized omission

Been harmonized to

Been to look up

to
Look up to appeal

Had your moving harmonized to

For grasping open your look up
To allure you moving

For gasping open your
Look up to allure

had your moving
Been

moving

Had you moving

Been living it

Look

No sound looks up
To no omission

Would look up
To no omission

Remembered end acted upon
For gasping open your

mouth
Grasping open
For grasping open your mouth

Just would in grasp chord

For close your gasping

Grasping foreclose your mouth

For grasping open your mouth

For gasping
Open your mouth

Just would in grasp chord

Just would out gasp

Just would in gasp
chord

With strength in security ends

tremor
Trembling strength in security ends

Would

Ends

hands

With strength indecision ends

Trembling hands

Tremoring chord your
Would

Tenoring chord your

Been chorus overheard
Tenoring chord
Would

Word
Would

by

without

Been porous on without

Been porous by without

Been porous on without

Had your body
Been porous by without

Been porous on without

Prompt

Who you have continually overheard
Knotted up small movements
And mumbling to you hear
And hats
Which you wear really
As what you headed toward you
Saturate through in vision
Lifting up unvocalized to you hear in
The scene rips through
And overhead
And sew

Prompt

And overhead and sew

Lifting up unvocalized to you hear in
To so blend overhead

And mend
And sew

Lifting up unvocalized to you hear in
The scene rips through
And sew

The scene rips through
And overhead
And sew

You dry

Which overhead
And mend porous to you hear
And sew

Pores rendered quietly

Lifting up unvocalized to you hear in
That
The scene rips through
And sew
You rendered

Rendered over
And rendered over

And sew

And overhead

The scene rips through
And overhead
And rendered
And sew

And pours really mended
And sew

The scene rips through
And overhead
And pours mended
Dry you

Mended

Blend dry through you

And dry you

The scene rips through
And overhead
And pours really blended
You dry

mend pores really
Through you to lay dry

The scene rips through
And overhead blended
And pours really
Through you dry

And overhead
And porous really mended
You dry

you
Porous really mended through you
dry

And overhead blended
Pours really

sew up

And sewn up

Stitched

mend pores really
And dry
Still

And mend pores really
Through you to lay dry

And mend you pores really
Through you stay dry

Mended you pores

ous really

And really blended you pores

And pores really blended you

The scene rips through
And overhead
And mend pores really
Through you to lay dry

In the scene rips through

The scene rips through
Quietly mending

overhead

Overhead mended

Overhead quietly mending

Through overhead quietly mended

Lifting up unvocalized to you hear
In the seam ripped head

In the scene to be stripped
rips over

Lifting up unvocalized to you hear in
The scene to be rips over

seam rips over

In the scene rips over

In the seam to be ripped over

Over hat

Lifting up unvocalized to you hear
That dripping

As what you headed toward you saturated
Lifting up unvocalized to you hear
Over that seen dripping

As what you headed toward you saturated
Lifting up unvocalized to you hear
Over that seen ripping

Lifting up unvocalized to you hear
Over you seam that dripping

Saturated unvocalized light
Lifting you up
To you hear

of air

Your breathing in your ear

Saturated unvocalized light
Lifting you up
To you hear
Your breathing in your ear
Is you material

The hat

Breathing material
Of course not

The cartilage in your ear

Breathing material

To catch your breathing

Heavy breathing with your ear
Worn materially

Perking you up
To you hear

Lifting you up

Pepping you up

As what you headed toward you
Saturated unvocalized light
To you hear

sun even
Unvocalized to you hear

Saturated sun
Even unvocalized to you hear

As what you headed toward you
Saturated with sun even
Unvocalized to you hear

As what was headed toward you
Upgrading yourself

As what was headed toward you
Hoist yourself up
With the sun vocalized to you

Lifting yourself up with even
The sun vocalized to you

Lifting yourself up with even
The sun vocalized to you hear

loose
Vocalized to you hear
Loose

to you hear

you hear

hear

Lifting yourself
Up with even the sun vocalized loose
To you hear

With even the unvocalized to you hear

And hats
Which you wear really
As what you said
As what you headed for you

said
Headed for you

As what headed for you

As what you headed for you

And hats
Which you wear really
As what was said
As what was headed for you

As what you said
As what you headed for you

What was said
What with what was headed for
Comforting it can be so all your

All yours

As what was said
As what with what was headed for you

As what you said
As what you headed for

Comforting it can be so all your

you

And hats
Which you wear really
As what was said
As what was headed for you

With what's said
What with what was headed for you

Which you wear really
What with what was said
Headed for you

what was said
What with what was headed for you

What was said

Comforting it can be all yours

What was said
What with what was headed for
Comforting it can be all yours

your

o all

Which you wear really
What with what's said
What with what's headed for
Comforting it can be all your

All but yours

What was said
What with what was headed for
Comforting it can be so small
All but yours

All yours

All yours

Which you wear really
What was said
What with what
Was headed for

Comforting it can be so all yours
What with what
Was said

What with what

All yours
For comforting it can be so small

tall

It can be all your comfort
For comforting it can be so small

What was said
What with what was headed for
Comforting it can be so
All yours

And hats
Which you wear really
What was said

What with what was headed for
Comforting it can be so all yours

It can be all your comfort
For comforting it can be so small

And mumbling to you hear
And hats

And hats
And mumbling to you wear

And mumbling you wear

And hats

And acts you wear

And speaking you wear
And hats

And acts you wear

And hats
And acts you wear speaking

Present Surround

Who you have continually overheard
In tall weeds and past yourself
Confirm up incrementally
Through you can streak grass
And air in traces
Diminish with you around
That access inside leaving
Refuse ephemerally
In supporting you proceed
And blend awning over
Present surround

Present Surround

Cast present surround

And blend awning over
Cast to develop

Impart to develop

To cast to develop

Excess you develop

And blend awning over
Excess to develop

Formation that develops

Excess and develop

Excess to develop

In supporting you proceed
And blend awning over
To be covered

And blend awning over
Access you develop
And churn view

And blend awning
And churn later

And blend awning over
And churn view

And turn view

In supporting you proceed
With churn under awning

And blend later

And blend under awning
And churn later

And blend view

And reflect

And churn later

With plain view

And bend under awning
To blend view

In supporting you proceed
And blend under awning
And bend view

To blend under awning
And view

With viewing

And blend under mineral

With view

In supporting you proceed
And blend under interval
With view

And bend under interval

And blend under

And blend under interval

under blending

With roost blending over

With root bending under

In supporting you proceed
And roost blending over

And notice blending

And roosted over

And roost blending over

In supporting you proceed
With minerals

With minimal bending over

With time bending over

To cede view

In supporting you
To time bending over
Cede view

Refuse ephemerally
In supporting you proceed
With time bending over
To cede view

With spine bending over
Cede view

Though in time bending over

Refuse ephemerally to concede

Refuse ephemerally
In supporting you recede

Refuse ephemerally you recede

you concede

In view

To respond you can seed
And tall weed

To support you can seed

Refuse ephemerally to concede

To support you can seed

In supporting you can seed

To cede your view

To concede your view minimally

To your view minimally

That stem inside leaving
Refuse ephemerally to concede

Refuse ephemerally in support

That stem inside leaving

That stem inside leaves
Refuse you in support

In supporting you can seed
And

In responding you concede

Refuse ephemerally
In supporting you concede

In support of you concede

Refuse ephemerally
In responding you can cede

And

In supporting you can seed
And

Supporting can seed
And

Refuse ephemerally
In supporting can cede
And

To you can cede

Refuse ephemerally in supporting you

can cede

That stem inside leaving refuse
Ephemerally in supporting you

can cede

Refuse ephemerally in support
View can cede

You can cede

Refuse ephemerally
In supporting you can cede

In support can be viewed

In supporting you can cede
In supporting view

Refuse ephemerally
In support review

That stem inside leaving
Refuse ephemerally in support

To view minimally and reflect

Refuse minimally can respond

Which diminish with you around
That stem inside leaving
Refuse minimally can respond

Outlines minimally can reflect

To view minimally and reflect

As view minimally

For view minimally can reflect

That stem inside leaving
View minimally can reflect

Though cede you can reflect

To cede view can reflect

Through view can posit around

That stem inside leaving
With you can posit around

With you can be rotated around

With view can be rotated

When you can be reflected
That stem inside leaving

For view can be reflected

And stirred view can reflect

And cede view to reflect

To view can cede outward

And cede you can look outward
That stem inside leaving

To growth inside leaves stirred

To growth aside leaves stirred

Which diminish with you around

In turned

In terms lightly fused

In turn likely fused

Which diminish around you

And air in traces
Which diminish around you boost

And air in traces
Diminishing around you boost

In terms lightly fused
In terms likely fused

Diminishing around you

boost

In turn lightly and sayable

In turn both lightly and soil

Diminishing around you booth

Both in turn lightly in soil
In turn both lightly in soil

In turn both light and soil

And air in traces
With diminishing around you boost

Which diminishing around you churn

In lightly contribution

And air in churn
Which diminishing you traces

And air in traces
Which diminish in you boost

Which diminishing around you
In churn

Diminishing around you boost

In turn

Diminishing around you booth
In churn

And air in traces

Diminish in sight

Which diminish going around

Which diminish growth around

In churn

And air in traces
In churn around to you light

In churn around you to

In churn around you lightly

And air in traces

Diminish around you

And air in traces

diminished

And diminish traces

And dissolve
Then look

sayable

look sayable

and can look around

Fallow then can look around
And fallow then can look around
Tracing

wonder

traced under

left under

undo

through

Fallow than can be tracing

Fallow in places

And blocked light in traces

Which is in traces

In Contact

End

And end

By past will

Hand talking
By past will

Tend

And talking by

And walking by

By fast will

Hand

Finding view

Or you by talking

For you by talking

Close up

Hand talking by

With incompletely
Finding view

To be
Close up

Or face

In talking

To be close up

By talking

To be close
Up by talking

Up by face

By you talking

In you by talking

By you

And talking by

And walking by

And in face

Finding view
To be close

And face filled

With incompletely
Finding view

To be close
Or face

For here instance

To be close
For here face

To stretch over
Or close
Or face

To be close
Or sketched over
Or face

To be close
Or sketched
Or face

To be sketch over
Or close
Or face

To be sketched
Over face

In contact
To be close
Or face

To be close

In contact
Stretched over
Or face

Finding view

From that instance
Finding view

For that instant

Or face

To be
Stretched

Finding view

sketched
In that instance

Or face

To be close

Near that mouth
From here instance

Finding view
In that mouth

With incompletely
Finding view
From here
In that

Or face

With incompletely

Finding view
From here

Audible

To be close

Finding view audible
In here

With incompletely
Finding
View audible

Or face

With incompletely
Finding view convert

Inaudible here

To be close

Or face

Finding view convert

With incompletely
Finding view

Audible

To be close

And register for you
With incompletely
Binding view

Act

Binding view
Act

With incompletely
Binding contact

Finding view

Or face

Project

Project with incompletely

Binding view
Project with
Incompletely

binding

Project with incompletely

Binding
View incompletely

And register for you
Incompletely binding
Little thing

Or face

Incompletely binding
Little things
With

Incompletely binding
With little things

And register for you
Incompletely finding
Little things

To be close

And register for you
Binding little thing

With contact

Contract with little things

Contact
With little things

Little fleeting
With contract

And register for you
Little fleeting
With contact

Or face

Little things
Contract

Little thing

With contact

And register for you
Little thing

Fleeting between

Little thing
Between

And register for you
Little thing
Fleeting

Little thing

Between

And register for you

Have here
Little thing

Contract
Between

To be close

Have here

With little thing
Fleeting

Little thing
Between

And register for you

Have here

Little
Between

Or close
Fleeting

Little thing

Or close

Between

Or face

Little things

And register for you

Have here

Fleeting

Have here
As usually have

Have here as usual

Between

Caught up have here

Have here
Caught up within facing

And register for you

face

And register for you

face

And register for you face

And register
For you face

To in that bare sense

Register

For you face

To be close

And between view

For you face

To in that bare sense

And between view

Register before

And you face

To in that bare sense

Registered before

And you

To in that bare sense

Registered before you

Which is trying

To in that bare sense

Or face

Registered before

To in that bare sense

Emit matter to converse

Which is trying

To in that bare sense

Emit matter to converse

Notes

A portion of "Hum With" appeared in *Conundrum* and was initially written for the catalogue of the "Oops, I did it again!" exhibit at Chicago's 1926 gallery.

A portion of "Prompt" appeared as letter-press object on Answer Tag Home Press and as a broadside on Portable Press at Yo-Yo Labs. The entire poem was published as a chapbook by the Chicago Poetry Project.

"Present Surround" was included in the *DC Poetry Online Anthology 2004*.

"In Contact" grew from my interaction with members of the Council for Jewish Elderly's Adult Day Service and is dedicated to these individuals, the workers and families serving them, and any people suffering from Alzheimer's or dementia resulting from other conditions. The poem was published as a chapbook by Answer Tag Home Press.

Thank you very much to the editors of the above publications, and to my friends, for encouragement and invaluable dialogue. A particular thanks to Leonie Weber, Mark Booth, Jeff Clark, and Patrick Durgin.

Who Opens, by Jesse Seldess
ISBN: 0-9767364-0-3
Published by Kenning Editions

(c) 2006 by Jesse Seldess

Order from Small Press Distribution
1341 Seventh Street, Berkeley CA 94710
www.spdbooks.org
1-800-869-7553

See also: www.durationpress.com/kenning

The publication of this book has been made possible, in
part, by the generosity of the following donors to Kenning
Editions: Charles Bernstein, Susan Schultz, Lyn Hejinian,
Marcia Hofer, Marcia Pevsner, David Pavelich, Adalaide
Morris, Barbara Guest, Kevin Killian, Norma Cole, Pierre
Joris, and Alan Golding.